Vines

Overpower

Trellis

and

Run

Vines

Overpower

Trellis

and

Run

Claudia McGill

Other Books by Claudia McGill

Poetry:

Look Winter in the Face
Spring Cleaning
Catch Up With Summer
Autumn Opens a Door
Twenty Minutes
Get to the Point
Enough For a Book
Compositions in Collage
Picking Up Pieces
Picture Making
Refuge
Generous With the Details
Repairs
Redirection
Rearrange
Clean Canvas

Other Works:

The Journey to Survival: The Search for Moral Self-Awareness in the Works of Joseph Conrad (literary criticism)

Distractions Can Be Murder (mystery novel)

Introduction

These tiny poems are written according to a formula —
each one must have three lines, or maybe four, but no
more.

That's it.

I write them in groups (there is a table at the back of
the book that lists them by date) and I do it this way:

- To prepare for a session, I take notes —
  conversations, TV dialogue, ads on the radio. I
  don't discriminate or edit, I just write down
  phrases or sentences that I hear.

- When I'm ready to write, I take out my notebook
  and I make a list of appealing fragments. It's
  better to have too many rather than too few
  choices.

- Then I start to combine them. I use additional
  lines from my notes, or I fill in my own lines.

- When I've done enough, I stop.

It's best not to overthink the process. I don't go back
and work over the finished poems — it seems to take
the clarity and bite away from them. In pretty much
every case, second-guessing and rewriting only remove
the zing. I certainly don't want that. Instead, I move on
to a new set of poems when I want to say more.

I call these poems "Little Vines", from the word *vignette*.
I thought *vignette* was too fancy; I liked the
straightforwardness of these two words - Little Vines.

Now that I think about it, I guess it is funny that I am
using the word *straightforward*, as these Vines are
twisty, like all vines are. They go places, they find a
way, and they get there fast, but they are not –
straightforward.

Well, I'll leave it to you to read them and work your
way though the turns and tangles. See what you think.

Claudia McGill
June 2018

Vines

Overpower

Trellis

and

Run

1.
I must speak to my family.
So many stories I can't talk about.
Compulsive lying helps me focus.

2.
I missed you so much.
You did not notice I was gone.
Don't make me chase you.

3.
That girl was
special ordered
leafy thin fashion perfect

4.
cake on a plate
silverware rattles
breakfast is on the table

5.
ghosts
working their way into his dreams
fish floating belly-up in guilt

6.
tropical storm
in my head
splitting it in two

7.
Forget the medicine
I don't recommend it
OK, I'll call you after the funeral service

8.
So I show up here passed out
It's medicinal I swear
and I quit cigarettes months ago.

9.
I can't keep doing ten percent safe
That's not the future I had in mind.
I'm ok but I wake up thinking

10.
The baby won't stop crying
I slapped a book
instead.

11.
A conversation explosion
even the quiet ones interrupting
a story too preposterous to be a lie

12.
You'd be in jail right now if it weren't for me
She said you pushed her
Perhaps you should have.

13.
What can you do after you finally
subpoena her bank records
and she skips out on Thursday's bus

14.
I've devoted years of work
to the family
trapped here in a squeaky-clean kitchen

15.
account full of stolen money
a little adrenaline flowing
international finance is very tiring

16.
The stars told me
the end of the story from the beginning
but I don't think the paperwork is done

17.
Maybe it corrected itself but
don't waste time analyzing
It's nothing radiation can't fix.

18.
There is some flabby rudeness in this room.
I extended my hand and you slapped it away.
I'd prefer a cordial but distant relationship.

19.
The color is off
undercooked by the look of it
Call the waiter. Call a lawyer.

20.
How dear of you to think of us
you jolly man addicted to breath mints
we will spend the money you left to us
as fast as we can.

21.
all the items you have not thought of for years
decided to call up out of memory
this one last time

22.
You know the holiday spirit disappears
a couple of hours before the mall closes.
Don't tell me to calm down.

23.
No place you'll ever want to go
Follow the smell
The entrance is in the back.

24.
Is it possible on short short notice
to leave the job half-finished
I apologize and I am glad we understand each other.

25.
Slap the thief into the ambulance
take him to the hospital
He fell into the trophy case and got all cut up.

26.
Make the call.
Has sorry come your way yet?
Your second chance is walking off.

27.
A decent human being
doesn't hold grudges
Move the car, you heard the man

28.
What a vexing attitude
it won't budge a piece of cake
it's an apology cut into slices.

29.
Money laundering
don't be ashamed of it
think of it as redecorating

30.
You are going to have to play ball
Defy me and you'll regret it
Go ahead, put some heart into it.

31.
Now he's walking off
such a sneaky liar and he needs a good talking to
I hope he doesn't slip and fall and break both legs.

32.
Are you sure it's a good idea
to claim ownership
of four crates full of ideas

33.
Mopping the floor with the paintings
might not be the smartest thing to do
in a museum

34.
Erase the lines on the page
you've accomplished nothing
truth serum will reveal what I need to know

35.
why did you let her
get her hands on
your memories

36.
I've got his wallet
eight years since it disappeared
I found it behind the radiator

37.
fighting in the back yard
what's a washed-up guy like you
thinking?

38.
a new pen made enemies
arrested for making threats
chewed up the paper until only shreds were left.

39.
Defy me and you'll regret it
Buy the best gift possible
and give it to me.

40.
sipping champagne
playing pool
in the rec room over the garage

41.
A profoundly bad man
in a subtle kind of way
Take a look through his sunglasses.

42.
Cold feet running for cover
they get into the car and drive away fast
One headlight has burned out.

43.
tomorrow morning first thing
fresh air change of scenery
I have earned that second chance

44.
sitting at the table in the restaurant
coffee spilled on the table
eyes full of expensive tears

45.
No better time to clean house
as she plucked a piece of broken glass
from her hair

46.
broken feelings broken plate
what's the difference
it's just a little one-act play.

47.
old memories punish you
until you short-circuit
you must find the off switch

48.
the last words in the book are
what is he selling and how much will it cost
double-check your wallet

49.
rich man wearing a big ring
glancing at a huge gold watch
anxious to try a new bad habit

50.
you sent a sentimental greeting card
and a faux-leather pen case
I see I'm not very high on your list.

51.
a shoebox of old letters
full of surprises
that were on the spicy side

52.
vacation snapshots
of canoes full of Girl Scouts on a camping trip?
That's your business, I guess.

53.
I have a jealous imagination
I don't soft-pedal the ugly truths
I know some answers, believe me.

54.
who can compete
with a convoluted story like that
no brain can be expected to do that much

55.
the employees got a bonus
spent it on coffee and new cars
now it's back to hard hats and work shirts

56.
my poor aching muscles
strumming like a ukulele
I can't fall asleep

57.
does it matter whose idea it is?
let's talk like the enemies we are
let's take off the gloves.

58.
every cubic inch of your existence
has been charted out but
it's hard to imagine they gave you no friends at all

59.
a bolt of lightning
an electrical circuit
grinning and showing a lot of teeth

60.
I finish writing this note to old friends
by the end of it
we are no longer friends

61.
I ask you, my friends the flying insects,
how about a small slice of cake?
It's my secret recipe.

62.
spatter paint or
pick a number
you decide

63.
three innocent kittens
the equivalent of two cups of white sugar
in sweetness

64.
we will find out if anyone is serious
about caring for the small blue snails
afflicted with radioactivity

65.
your foolishness with a knife
hasn't helped us make any new friends
since we came to town

66.
the whining
you taught me the basics
but I'm certainly no expert

67.
Hello, needle in a haystack
I'm so proud of you
No one's found your exact address

68.
four hundred very scared eggs
looking for a clean start
No restaurant work, please.

69.
don't go chasing down the street in this heat
just put it in your purse
and look for a cab

70.
I barely knew him
I just didn't like him telling the truth
Send him back to where he came from.

71.
My mind a nexus of all memories
I can see inside the veins of a leaf
but my emotions are a mystery to me

72.
the pattern is random
the brain waves
blew a hole in it

73.
it was the last thing anyone expected
the lightning strike was not fatal
we are all disappointed

74.
it was perfectly respectable
some sort of vegetable transfusion
to modify my behavior

75.
your alter ego
reflected in a mirror
now I know why your jealousy is so intense

76.
discount prices are compelling
intruding on my mental peace
things looking grim but still plenty manageable

77.
a broken toe
out-numbered two to one
by a stiff knee and damage to the garage

78.
call the doctor and get his opinion
of the scales on her nose
don't just assume it is fate

79.
you don't have to explain yourself but
who knows why you do half the things you do
I suppose it's just instinct

80.
no injury to anyone except
a small green spider
in a china tea cup

81.
there is no plot
it's all nonsense
and at the same time very understandable

82.
the babysitter tipped her off
the message was in code
don't you love the feeling of danger?

83.
I just hope
they were at the movie theater all afternoon
not out breaking the law

84.
it's a theory that travels from place to place
a dozen eggs waiting to become chickens
what do you make of it?

85.
outnumbered
at the orphanage
you must keep your mouth shut

86.
We keep a close eye on everyone
we match the pieces together
Sometimes we have to stop remembering.

87.
Why am I even here?
I'm here for the coffee
and the nightmare visions that come with it

88.
do you know how much trouble I'm in
owing three years of back taxes
I tell you what, you panic or you focus

89.
yelling at the neighbors
you know what it's like
no drama just routine

90.
It is your fault
the future is in the tea leaves
and you just threw them out

91.
I am cleaning up this mess
I'm not negotiating
The wedding's off

92.
chainsaws and industrial pesticides
you said it was a medical emergency
I said it'll be a new start

93.
the owl in the solid black dark
blinking its eyes
full of secrets

94.
I thought you had been suffocated
there was a story a while back
I guess you can't take gossip that seriously

95.
I was trying to be smart
I studied algebra
but it was just too little too late

96.
you keep pushing him
he is the only one with the answer
he is self-diagnosed with forgetfulness.

97.
well, you haven't broken any laws
disappointing but not surprising
your first time out on your own

98.
Look at me there in the mirror
Do you see decay and futility of effort?
No, it's just a skin rash.

99.
taken to the top floor
pushed off the balcony
since when are we astronauts?

100.
the scenery
a shining ribbon of blur
at sixty miles an hour

101.
all my memories
fading into the fog
guilt is all that's holding me together

102.
family problems
nausea and supernatural connections
the paramedics are on the way

103.
there's been an incident
talk to your lawyer
remember, you are an entirely honest person

104.
life is short
life is a postcard
learn shorthand

105.
I've figured it out.
Failure:
That street is full of one-way traffic.

106.
get enough of that panic and fear
your stomach pushes off hard
does a double flip and does it again

107.
a leaf fell too early
can anybody
make it count for something

108.
What with the T-shirts, food poisoning, and skeletons
it's so important to keep the door locked
in this stupid town

109.
this is not supposed to be my life
a guide paid by the hour
spouting out slogans

110.
built a one-way street
blocked every exit
didn't answer phone calls
couldn't stop remembering

111.
if you're wondering
there have been a couple of fights
and not a lot of big-picture thinking

112.
sweeping out the garage
it's a legal activity
There's no reason you can't do it too.

113.
petty criminals here in town
owe me some money
it means a lot of people are making mistakes.

114.
the paid informant
ears twitching
all the way across town

115.
rules for you and rules for everybody else
the whole thing reeks
Get out your checkbook. Payment's due.

116.
coming home with other people's jewelry
he might have a dozen good reasons
but that fixation is going to cost him

117.
stumbles and staggers
unsure rhythms
etched across her face□

118.
She kept everything in those boxes.
Never letting go had its price.
I call it revenge of the passive.

119.
No more detours left
out there on this road.
This is the last exit.

120.
By the way
do you remember my sister?
The end of that story was such a disappointment.

121.
I am your guide
the person you have been waiting for
exotic and sharp as a tack

122.
here in the kitchen
have a beer why don't you
we are home again.

123.
If it is a punishment you are waiting for
it is sitting in a pew three rows back.
Eventually you will have to look behind you.

124.
A lady removing fingernail polish
removing the magic
and who asked you to look

125.
Sitting in front of the television
catching up on paperwork
taking notes on feeling sorry for myself

126.
headache never letting go
nerves stretched out skinny
need aspirin need one hundred aspirin

127.
tell the truth and it will make no difference
you will float downstream face-down
no matter what.

128.
Slipped on three hundred dollars' worth of bananas
ruined an expensive pair of shoes
it's just not funny anymore

129.
Counting it twice
That's the nonsense you want to sell me
That's your money-laundering technique?

130.
which one is the decoy
the fiction
the lie
the story?

131.
Let's split up and search the back yard
It's not what you thought but something else
worse.

132.
Four hours and poison at the end of it?
What kind of training session
did you think you were attending?

133.
Not you again
with your stupid jokes
What happens when a dull pencil meets paper?

134.
had specific reasons
told hundreds of lies
insane or just moving a little too fast
you can decide

135.
I spent a lot of money on that car
so stop that happy talk
and get a tow truck

136.
of course your gray suit is still at the cleaners
I have better things to do
than to steal laundry

137.
I fell flat on the floor
Three days in the hospital
weak, drunk, and suffering from a full-body rash.

138.
The new prescription isn't helping
I've been told
a nice little operation might do the trick

139.
Flowers arrived
half-dead
and no card was enclosed.

140.
The miserable old hypocrite
styling himself
the enemy of insipid thought

141.
I typed this letter screaming and crying
and as if that weren't enough
suffering from a bad cold

142.
I'm ending this particular friendship
I no longer want to
make a visit to the reformatory every Sunday.

143.
start a new life forget the old life
start remembering the day before yesterday
when I believed you and I paid your bail

144.
good intentions
worn down like old shoes
forced down too many rough roads□

145.
he is a very handsome man but jealous
every hair split right down the middle
five hundred years of therapy couldn't help him

146.
what with the gambling
guess he left town owing some money
you won't find that low-life vermin crawling back home
          any time soon

147.
I took up the guitar
He was always laughing at me
I made sure he fell down the stairs.

148.
To lie and cheat and steal from here into next week
I never asked for things to be like this
Now that they are, I kind of like it.

149.
I tried everything and nothing worked.
I was accused of negligence but I got off with
          a reprimand.
Your hair will grow back.

150.
The doctor is with a patient
intent on testing a hypothesis
regarding revenge of the passive.

151.
blank pages in a notebook
a pair of broken eyeglasses
and no memory of what had happened

152.
empty plates on the table
something burning in the oven
my stomach is starting to get suspicious

153.
You want excitement?
Let's get down to the kitchen
and set the dishtowels on fire.

154.
a cymbal in each hand
There will be a lot of ruined music
and terrified little eardrums that don't understand

155.
a stack of books on money laundering
a briefcase full of money
looks like we're no longer powerless frauds

156.
Do you like fruit juice
or are you a beer drinker?
I count three votes for and one against.

157.
Good thing the lamp shorted out.
I decided right then
I'd divorce her.

158.
You know what people are saying
Was it an accident
that thing with the poisoned lunch meat?

159.
Any chance you could shoo that fly away?
That isn't a social call he's making
to the sugar bowl.

160.
That's an expensive lipstick
Seven deadly sins in seven minutes
No jury would convict.

161.
Your application rejected
The embarrassment and the insult.
It really was very funny.

162.
What tasteless joke?
Twenty thousand safety pins and a fistfight
and you're disappointed?

163.
for crying out loud
of course things have changed
Wake up and smell the rotten potatoes.

164.
Thank you for your discretion
the mistake was in thinking nothing will change
That much kissing sends a message.

165.
never lifted a shovel in his life
a huge splinter in his thumb
where is that very proud man now?

166.
The orchestra playing a selection
from the soundtrack of that popular movie
"The Self-Respecting Blunt Force Blow"

167.
stabbed in the heart with a safety pin
surgery scheduled for next week
resting comfortably but still holding a grudge

168.
people were not lining up for the chance
to grow up in an orphanage
last I heard

169.
in the concert hall singing sweet revenge
their voices
broken glass on the ground

170.
Dusting the shelves.
The stars said it can't wait.
Better not disappoint them.

171.
The quiet life you want so badly -
looking for a missing button
burning the toast and running out of butter

172.
Your eyesight managed to confuse you
the benefit of an improved mood.
Cut back on the drinking.

173.
was it sugar or salt
the thought of it
too much for his sanity

174.
she kept a diary,
perhaps a bad idea.
he blackmailed her.

175.
It might be risking your reputation but
it wouldn't hurt you to smile
Let me buy you a drink at the club.

176.
You humiliated the poor man
a decent man in spite of everything
and it's nothing a good pair of tweezers wouldn't fix

177.
The growling dog scratching at the door
just trying to relive all those good memories.
Never drop your guard.

178.
Insatiable appetite for glass-shattering loud music
It's no good appealing to her conscience
Try on the earplugs instead.

179.
sweaty muscular men
screaming and in quite a state
it was beyond embarrassing

180.
the hospital is full of people who are full of germs
try not to be so shocked
years and years it's been that way

181.
lying on the carpet
lying on the sidewalk
lying on the floor of the shower
Stop lying.

182.
I know exactly who I am
a symbol of confusion
the innuendos you try to swat away

183.
A very charitable family but
bear in mind that rat poison
can strain ties.

184.
An argument about missing money
glowing infrared-hot.
I'd bet on embers and sparks and bridges
        being burned.

185.
A social-climbing set of narcissists.
An insatiable appetite for mayhem.
Sorry to interrupt your committee meeting.

186.
You're up so early
you obnoxious troublemaker
You took me by surprise.

187.
I'm not ignoring you I just don't like you
I am
a ruined landscape covered in leafless trees

188.
The cake baking competition.
Milk of magnesia and pain killers.
I'm not really feeling up to much right now.

189.
It's not that nice here
everyone cries
a fresh batch of tears every week

190.
Is he drunk, your uncle
or is this
a homemade therapy session

191.
She needs to forgive her no-good husband
Now you're talking crazy
Cut him out of the will, more like it.

192.
Intention versus action
twice in one day
Now the old lady expects an apology

193.
He had a new girlfriend who smelled bad.
She was a nobody
with a substantial sum of money in the bank.

194.
The ideal high school student
and a bonfire in the backyard. Dad said
Listen, you haven't been smoking, have you?

195.
the astral plane
has landed on the moon
the pilot eating a chili dog

196.
The cake is just lovely.
A toast to all the red silk neckties.
A long life to all you pompous old men!

197.
Magic gone wrong just one time and now
an old man smoking a pipe
in the baby's crib

198.
My visions have brought great suffering
romantic entanglements and conspiracy theories.
I pull a giant rabbit out of a very tiny hat.

199.
I am anemic in the dark
Hope keeps me up at night
Consider this a call from the void.

200.
a sprained right ankle
three stitches in my arm
after some rest and a course of rabies shots I will
        be fine.

201.
our cousin lives with us
the visitor who dropped in and never left
ignore him and he will go away they said.
it was not true.

202.
he was an attractive and successful man
he has very loyal friends and a total lack of character
typical just typical

203.
a sour expression squeezed dry
a quart of vinegar wrung out of it
maybe things will look more cheerful in the morning

204.
a fit of temper and it all went to pieces
the age difference was no barrier
to a good knockdown drag-out fight

205.
honest, nobody knew
but with a little bit of guesswork
a number of people can barely look me in the eye

206.
he was a capable surgeon, all right
too drunk to drive home
complications from a broken tibia is the least of
        his concerns

207.
arguing and more arguing
they'll appear in court next week
it would be a shame to waste those harsh words

208.
unstable charming woman
pushing a wheelbarrow full of
such hostility such dark looks

209.
you were too hasty and you did a slipshod job
now you have a business associate
with an ice-pack on his knee

210.
I might spill the beans or I might not
Call the florist who delivered the flowers
if you must crack the mystery of the secret admirer

211.
two plane tickets to somewhere
shock scraped the smile off her face
write her a check and push her out the door.

212.
all those years ago you lied to me
forgiveness is easy if you didn't care much to start with
But I did. I hope your insurance is paid up.

213.
Let's meet here tomorrow
and we can make the same mistake again?
An extreme view but appealing all the same

214.
ever since he married my sister
she is plenty tough
did I mention he has super-sensitive ears?

215.
he wore his pants too tight
she had a bad reputation and a difficult home life
everything is complicated by a lack of money

216.
she does not approve
she doesn't buy it
But I think it's dynamite with extra-sharp teeth

217.
a know-it-all little troublemaker
with a suitcase full of dirty clothes
I feel for you but I'm losing patience

218.
she saw me waiting in the parking lot
a cheese sandwich in my lunchbox
but she didn't have to know that

219.
A lifetime in a dark tunnel
not waking from the nightmare
I've seen the ghosts. I will set myself free.

220.
your emotional hurricanes
certainly have stirred things up
I'm dreading the next few pages in this book.

221.
Let me pretend to give you some advice
People are noticing things
and new policy says we must take photos.

222.
I need something with real stopping power
Poison might not do the job
I'm considering four different kinds of chili pepper.

223.
I took the hint from the barber
He earned a certificate in interpreting tarot cards.
Be careful going down the stairs.

224.
Push her right out the door
Set yourself free
Don't be sorry to be so selfish

225.
A romantic issue
I'd say about six more months will tell
if you can pick back up where you left off

226.
Your power to incinerate a clear glass of cold water:
Impressive clarity and certainty of purpose.
Help yourself to world domination.

227.
Steal a car and run over a man
and you want my permission?
Go ahead, knock yourself out

228.
Am I still alive
or am I just a face in the mirror?
The skin protects a soul in pain.

229.
What does it mean, you want to come home
So much has gone on. Be honest with us.
Can you choose to be a decent person again?

230.
For a critique of this crazy story,
I suggest
a very small scream

231.
Applaud the odd question.
Neglect to answer it.
A conspiracy of repairmen.

232.
I found a knife in the sock drawer
No fooling, it really works
Ask that guy scattered on the carpet.

233.
You're welcome to stay for a week but that's
        long enough
you listening to old music and crying all night
your vanity worn down all smooth and shiny
Thank you for coming home again, oh yeah.

234.
what a great variety of words you are using
what a lot of sleepless nights I'm going to have
        to endure
what possessed me to marry you?

235.
algebra in my nightmares
two unknowns in each equation
a full moon three times a month

236.
I stole a whole wardrobe of plaid wool pleated skirts
A crime of passion
It's good and it just gets better.

237.
fate or luck, I don't know which one is worse
parrot or goldfinch, what does it matter as long as
        it's a bird
soul or imagination, pretty soon you'll figure it all out

238.
the car is parked over at the shopping center
there were no claw marks or bites
your alibi checked out, didn't it

239.
fled for his life in a motorboat
we're laughing, just laughing
we always thought a manhunt would be a lot of fun

240.
wearing a long black coat
sitting on a stool at the counter
not about to pick up the check

241.
I realized it was all in my head
so I wrote a book
I was always a guy with possibilities

242.
in the darkness
one hundred small sounds of panic
cross mercy off the list

243.
He has only half a heart
cut quite a few souls into pieces
some people crawl back up the food chain but he won't

244.
complete silence
in the living room
filled with secrets

245.
reading the ledgers full of red ink
her long thin pale-blue fingers trembled
while a whole truckload-full of souls waited

246.
In the wrong hands
even a crockpot is dangerous
Ladle out some of that delicious paper pulp

247.
You didn't see me because I wasn't there
And I resented everything you said
even though I never heard it

248.
a cup of coffee and it's not the first time
we weren't exactly friends, you know
but I draw the line at blackmail

249.
Find that numskull
You know what they say
Wait until you see the pictures

250.
their digestive systems finely calibrated
they used a tuning fork turned toward the
        meat frequency
they stepped out looking for a square meal
guess where the missing chickens went

251.
stole his shoes
cut his socks in one-inch squares
I found out later she had a whole different plan
but I think this one worked fine

252.
the part-time priest
peeked into the soul
wiped it clean

253.
crying her eyes out
memories in a purse
a purse full of fading-value coins

254.
just sold the string of pink pearls
one step ahead of the police sketch artist
fingers crossed you'll never find out

255.
coins in the bottom of the punch bowl
I never gave up hope
I never stopped looking

256.
Ask the science teacher
about the green liquid in the punch bowl
My conscience is bothering me again.

257.
resurrect those deleted sentences
excavate the truth out of her
There are not enough sleeping pills on earth
to get her a good night's rest.

258.
add up quite a few small read-my-lips
subtract the long-winded explanations
the sum is: one substantial screamed-out demand

259.
So roll out the whole persona
the part-time social worker
maneuvered into a too-tight pair of support socks

260.
I wish I could remember to be sorry
for interrupting you
Of course I'm interested in your perspective for a
change

261.
one hundred percent of one hundred percent
is still not enough
I had hoped hallucinogenics would bring me peace.

262.
I don't remember complaining of memory loss
My guess is I bought a one-way ticket to surreal city.
Fingers crossed, it seems like home here.

263.
Threw the money on the dining room table
It came from my indoor treasure-hunting excursion
aka bank robbery

264.
I'm full of pink praise but I can't go any stronger
I no longer have a conflicted set of attitudes
I am a fully-realized dream-crusher.

265.
I bought size large by mistake
Only turned my back for two seconds
There it was, size large, in my shopping bag

266.
financial records and conversations
lots of people holding a grudge
never play golf with a guy in a suit

267.
The situation is preposterous
This isn't my funeral
I am much more important than the guy they're
        talking about
is something funny or are you just laughing?

268.
Never came out of the fog
it was getting exhausting
We got divorced last year

269.
I give you no names no info no song-and-dance
I'm on my way into trouble
Let's go and go fast.

270.
on the run for two years you miserable little ghost
you can come home now
the insurance policy paid off

271.
You'll see a telephone number on the side of a bus
call me and we'll talk business
when I come up for air

272.
You big lunk
If you believe what you just heard
there is a vacancy in the thought motel

273.
A gruesome state of circumstances
The patient is in surgery
Afterwards he will have to go into a new line of work.

274.
regain your balance
it's all in pieces
let me glue it back together

275.
them, the plotters and the schemers
us, guilty of nothing but being stupid
that's why we have insurance

276.
I have matching pairs of anxieties
I veto your idea
Twice.

277.
The eyes do their work
The hands make their choices
Isn't the future a fabric still to be woven?

278.
a big bald guy, that's the guy
a donnybrook in the laundromat
no one could get under my skin like he could

279.
people holding grudges
I am just a concerned citizen
dragging it all up again will be a lot of fun

280.
Blackmail used to be such a sure thing
but now no one is ashamed of anything
it's all good news and better news

281.
choking on a bite of public opinion
need not lead to social death
a good public relations person can fix you right up

282.
I'll lead the séance
my aunt is so superstitious
rest assured the spirits will make her understand

283.
I'll get my revenge
on the run
that kind of life never gets old

284.
a pipeline carrying dollar bills
right into my purse
turn up the flow and get me a suitcase

285.
the landlord disappeared
when repairs were needed
it's just basic self-defense

286.
some wealthy folks
some great big bloated cars
wait until they run out of gas

287.
four guys crammed in a too-small car
choose their own joyride
starting off today on an out-of-focus road trip

288.
kickbacks are a way of life
just you and me and the phone calls
and an awful big bank account

289.
crates of files in the basement
a mountain of paperwork
and no earthmover in sight

290.
we live in a city full of deja-vu
diverting tales and improper fabrications
worthless or priceless take your pick

291.
smuggling ring at the elementary school
they asked for a lawyer
So what if they're second graders

292.
she is a dangerous woman
her long red fingernails
clawing off the paint

293.
What's the point of being a harmless timid woman?
It is time for me to speak up
I'll be very careful to say the right things.

294.
tying up loose ends
the past happened to some other person
as gone as if it never existed

295.
It's useless teeth-gnashing
in a month or two
dumb and selfish is going to look good

296.
secretive and solitary and subtle
the pale and listless
in the nervous part of the day

297.
a tiny alarm clock
suffering from delusions
taking its revenge

298.
who are you and who have you become
resurrection and a second life
and maybe another one after that

299.
what a trite mind you have
it's a landslide of bad ideas
just what we need more of in this town

300.
a talent for understatement
keeping a low profile
Non-sequential unmarked bills.

301.
true or false
smiling is easier when you're cross-eyed
experts disagree.

302.
I like taunting you and I'll never stop
scatter a bit of faint praise
reach in and take you to pieces

303.
a hurricane on your wedding day
makes you wonder
is being married what you really want

304.
the cat hissed
bold in the daylight
impudent in the dark

305.
I'm just an old woman
eyes shut sitting in a rocking chair
listening to the sound of dirt against the shovel

306.
I waited and now I am finished waiting.
I have lied and now I am making it right.
I'll make bail for you and then we're square.

307.
you've spent the entire morning
staring through the bottom of the coffee mug
tell the ants your secret if you must tell someone

308.
there's a troublemaker in me
the itch is in my fingers
never get caught and never forgive

309.
a full moon and double vision
mistaken identity and too many rules
you wrote a letter and you got no answer

310.
listen to the sound of traffic
do you recognize the melody
maybe it's time to try something different.

311.
there is laundry in the bank
laundry in the laundromat
everybody's playing everybody else

312.
a head butt gets results
when you don't have time
for a crash course in sledgehammer swinging

313.
the mosquito chorus sweating it out
a crowd of riled-up loudmouths
out for blood

314.
the score is running up
a little more than I wanted to pay
Keep away from the high-five circus of office politics.

315.
The dialogue is sparse
daring you to step in
Don't do it.

316.
one fried egg
two reckless people
three kinds of fancy wallpaper

317.
forty-five tattoos
up for grabs
tore off down the street on a motorcycle

318.
crank up the fiction machines
you'll be buying a ticket for the moon tonight
a success story gone nova.

319.
the past has come back
driving a limousine
making an illegal left turn

320.
an abscessed molar and a doorknob
string yarn rope cord what's the difference
just so the knots are tight

321.
that idiot husband of hers
in the lobby and looking mighty worried
some things can't be fixed

322.
blame dropped out of the sky
fell right on to my head
things are getting messy all of a sudden

323.
too good at the job
never got caught
served you right

324.
the camera caught a smile
a snapshot of sophistication
the sheer unpleasantness of a conversation with her

325.
The alchemy of intimidation
it sure gets the job done
My goodness you do have a temper

326.
fly right up to the fifth floor
locate the exact center
crawl in through the loophole

327.
a friend dropped a hint
we are not passengers with the same itinerary
I'm afraid we must say adieu

328.
Working with a crew of dimwits and extortionists
certified members of the crazy fool association
every one of them with an off-center reputation:
I'd do it again in a minute

329.
She is deceitful and dangerous
surrounded by trusting souls
naïve satellites circling the perilous planet

330.
it's best not to think of it
a small dog
and some light hurried footsteps on the stairs

331.
rook and knight
with wrinkled foreheads
anticipate and reciprocate

332.
office full of gossiping clerks
made copies
shared secrets

333.
they wear cheap white shirts
ironed to starchy stiff scratchiness
why are they the way they are?

334.
it wasn't long ago I was just like you
frowning over the paperwork
a dim bulb in a wrinkled navy-blue skirt

335.
squeaky clean run-of-the mill office guy
inexpensive khaki pants
shredding documents at midnight

336.
How much do you really know about chemistry?
Maybe it was just fruit juice after all
At least remind me to send flowers.

337.
I could use the help of your
plausible and complicated
flexible thinking

338.
I added it up and it's not enough
a name plate on my desk and a pension
Maybe it's best not to think about it anymore.

339.
Not allowed
but helping themselves to the money
put the sparkle back into the office staff meeting

340.
harpoon the truth
give the wrench a turn
breathe just a little longer than the next guy.

341.
minimal truth-telling and
I always look for the exit.
I'm not a little girl anymore.

342.
two sides of the ledger
a tire blew and the car rolled
so now it's self-defense

343.
silence is not helping you
talk and talk good
don't skip a syllable of explanation

344.
What a colossal headache
you've turned out to be
And do you ever owe me a favor

345.
Surely I can do better than you
the conflict of necessity with availability
notwithstanding

346.
keep your distance from
the straight and narrow
lucky seven and we're done here

347.
soothe pinched words
check for bruised syllables
heal broken things

348.
slurred sentences healed
thoughts made clear
the asleep awakened

349.
I hear silence day and night
I remember all your names
I miss you

350.
Look at all that hairspray
enough to stun the local population
glue their feet to their bathroom floors

351.
a full moon and a pink sunrise
partners
on a scale unending and infinite

352.
bow ties and pin-tucked shirts
complacent smug smiles and beaded dresses
tiny shreds of conversational misery

353.
I should have kept my mouth shut
my teenage daughter
bugging my apartment and writing down the details

354.
this stuff is lethal
broccoli is poison to a junk food addict
who put you up to this?

355.
I know bribes and private deals tweak things
I don't want to be rude
I'd like to see a volume discount

356.
I have a hunch
you were popular in high school
I bet it said so on the syllabus

357.
a chartered airplane
OK, let's get it in gear
Look out for oncoming traffic

358.
the electrical wires heated up
poof
there went my hair-do

359.
you thought of everything
the secret encoded in the knitted pattern
the note behind the mirror in the Chinese restaurant

360.
the warmup to a long tirade
hold your breath and jump into a ditch
let it all pass over your head

361.
a double-cross in process
professionally done and high quality
nice to see her in trouble for a change

362.
You lummox
can you hear me
twirl the dial twice and try again

363.
it's the public library
where everyone shops for information
I'm not leaving until I get some answers.

364.
you knew what I was when you met me
my all-expenses-paid life story
typed out on a manual typewriter decades ago

365.
Spend an evening at the bowling alley
moonlighting as pin number eight
Being knocked out cold makes things easier

366.
struggling to acquire equilibrium
yellowing documents
may or may not reveal the old secrets

367.
I'll meet you in another life
I follow the footprints of people
who have long since walked out of sight

368.
tree spirits and phantasms
the broken-off key in the lock
I won't sleep a wink

369.
You lied to me
it was not really part of a cosmic plan
you dragged me into it now get me out

370.
don't know why and don't care how
I'm not a therapist I'm not a psychic
I'm the getaway driver

371.
I don't like eggs
I'd say you are couple of bad eggs
the least I can do is give you a good funeral
I fry eggs in a hot pan. Get in.

372.
it's Personnel but they call it Human Resources
        these days
a potent combination of inertia and team-building
authentic sheep in a pasture

373.
Two skinny ladies in leather leggings on a motorcycle
nothing left to lose reckless and smart
they can talk their way out of anything

374.
spill the guilt
sincerely
tastefully.

375.
imported mustard caught someone's eye
in the cafeteria kitchen
it's a long story, what happened next

376.
I need a really good fake driver's license
You're a real white knight coming to my rescue
Please don't make me look bad in the photo

377.
lunch in the cafeteria
usually smells like bleach and french fries
a pungent combination that gets attention

378.
dozens of eggs to make one big cake
it's the ultra-egg cake
it employs the egg as the front man

379.
We're on the clock now
I've already gotten the boss to pull out some of
        her hair
I shudder to think that I fit in here so well.

380.
I'm asking you to let it go
Put it away for good
it's time to move away from the edge of the cliff

381.
the mark has come into sight
there was a whole lot of screeching
our gal has certainly been quite an operator,
        hasn't she?

382.
an off-the-record catfight
it's all over except for the hair-pulling
even that is slowing down

383.
oh dear not another car accident
the car smashed like a carton of eggs
now the priority is finding a good mechanic

384.
Are you still pretending
we are telemarketers
I think it's more of a smash and grab operation

385.
Her ex-husband
jumped bail
The red tape just got to him.

386.
the meat mallet came in handy
and here I had thought we could be friends
believe me, it's your fault, not mine

387.
purchased a few dollars' worth of spray paint
next thing you know
these cufflinks really are gold, right?

388.
the radio drowned out the voices
of the two gods
emerging from the darkness

389.
so what's your angle
you foolish woman
are you sorry now or just inconvenienced

390.
a lovesick girl
lied to
don't turn your back on her

391.
the champagne is flat
the money is all gone
and you're whistling the same old tune

392.
I got good at taking orders
I don't leave loose ends
Forever is the end of this story.

393.
Let me see what's in that notebook
miles of words rolling down the pages
a flash flood we can't outrun

394.
he was newsworthy a decade ago
he outlived his luck
loose ends are being trimmed off now

395.
he couldn't find a needle in a pincushion
an anonymous tip and still no luck
Keep your chin up, pal

396.
until recently he was in the diplomatic service
top secret firmly shut and locked up tight
anonymous and good at it

397.
a feisty college dropout
a radio host with prominent front teeth
a reservation at the hotel

398.
Like a truck overturned on the highway
Like a workshop in selective destruction
but his heart was in the right place

399.
a mop of frizzy hair and a harmless smile
capable of an impressive amount of mayhem
pretzels would untwist themselves for her

400.
assuming that this man suspects nothing
the doctor has prescribed those big red pills
that should wrap things up ASAP

401.
harpoon the old memories
toss them off the apartment building from four
        stories up
a bird's eye view of good-bye

402.
better be sure you know the reasons
seven turned into twelve
help yourself to any words in the dictionary

403.
All I have to do is spread the word
about who's behind this little comedy
then touché, my friend, you disappear

404.
stop screaming you are attracting attention
jump inside the clothes dryer
I guess undercover work really doesn't suit you

405.
I live here all alone
I am in the one secure place
I quarantined myself to be safe from you

406.
I'm a minimalist
I don't know and I don't share
I just enjoy the quiet

407.
I wanted to see the world
a systematic eyes-peeled surveillance
three-continent tour kind of way

408.
a bruise on your forehead
you lost a whole mouthful of teeth
sounds like it was some kind of a party

409.
so what's your angle
where do you get all that hairspray
why is the government interested

410.
I am aware of crazy
I am aware of nefarious
though none of it bothers me now

411.
it was not a mistake to talk to you
your voice is easy to listen to
when you are saying something nice about me

412.
the girl wearing fishnet hose
where does she think she's going in that get-up
    I don't know
but she fried my heart like an egg in a skillet

413.
the bait
one morning
ambushed

414.
I bet no one has ever felt like celebrating
buck teeth and varicose veins
they are impossible to accessorize

415.
brainwaves in color
I don't make the rules
I take advantage of them

416.
fabrications in vivid color
poisoned conversation
I like knowing people like us.

417.
no need to ask twice
I'll stomp on that cockroach
then we'll call it even

418.
don't waste your sympathy on me
three husbands later
my bank account is finger-lickin' good

419.
any tips for this guilt-busting vigilante
over budget and behind schedule
still willing to do what it takes

420.
white collar criminals working on a schedule
putting in a lot of overtime hours
they're awfully good at doing what needs to be done

421.
I'd love to say I could help you
I thought you were my best friend
not a player in a game

422.
who is this man
disheveled and hungry
too ashamed to call home

423.
Your so-called fairy godmother
lying to you and a lot more than one time
I think you have grounds for a lawsuit

424.
Your dimwit brother-in-law
fell off the local scenic overlook
get over there right away and look sad

425.
counting on your fingers
between answers and no answers
confused by the jingle of your bangle bracelets

426.
no scent no sound no ripple in the air
I'm puddle-stomping angry
Get ready I'll be coming after you

427.
one digit and two fractions and three syllables
odd hours and random excuses
I'm starting to see a pattern

428.
a slithery blonde lady
the truth too heavy to carry by herself
singing like a canary now

429.
I'm shallow I accept bribes
I'm the person I want to be
Keep moving and don't look back at me

430.
all of a sudden he's out in the street
leading a busload of people
in an a cappella sing-along hootenanny

431.
she's back in town and now she wants to talk
her high-society ideas in the crossfire
her brainchild developing a headache

432.
wrestling a tiger in the center ring of the circus
I was out of practice and it showed
haunted eyes and shaking hands

433.
the stepbrother was the nervous type
leaped the fence
ran off full-tilt just like that

434.
Six months of international high jinks
My nerves a beer bottle smashed to pieces
I've reassembled myself back to normal now

435.
No family but plenty of sycophants
Lying was necessary
Sometimes you have to believe the lies.

436.
Currents of guilt take me
Tributaries flowing from all points of the compass
I am ready to accept my punishment

437.
the holiday party
a five-star survival course
I really threw myself into it

438.
I am convinced that lying is necessary
I spy on my friends
no wonder I don't trust you

439.
three dead husbands
a photo album for each one
Hold it right there, sister

440.
I see nothing wrong with what I am doing
I am very proud to say
the dealmaker is out and wheeling again

441.
poisoned conversation
put me in the hospital
the doctor seems like a nice guy but
it's lipstick that is keeping me alive

442.
some rowdy customers in the restaurant
who doesn't like a friendly scuffle?
I hope that man can rehabilitate his broken leg

443.
I know being happy is not my right
A second chance is
that crazy idea that made me hope

444.
in with a bad crowd, he was
he was not living in an aquarium
with a bunch of guppies

445.
I've seen that map
the consequences of never telling the truth
No one knows it like I know it

446.
she has a pert way of speaking
she lets drop a sleazy little innuendo or two
I'm not sure even you can keep your grandmother
        out of trouble

447.
genius by day
heroine by night
sassy talking at all hours

448.
a little off her game
one word ruined her reputation
it was over in seconds

449.
it's been a long time coming
it was icing on a cake
that was already plenty sweet

450.
her and her ideas
I think a good lawyer could get her off
if he works a lot of late nights

451.
a real old miser
a collection of silver coins
it's not just pocket change from under the seat cushions

452.
it's not against the law to speculate
suppose thick cardboard had been used instead
a lot of things would have been different

453.
one very strong guy
two kinds of thank you
three sets of books
Business as usual

454.
the high school principal
just going through the motions
no one listens to a pack of teenagers

455.
skip that one, give me the next one
I can't afford this kind of melodrama
Just choose a pork chop.

456.
couple of ladies
overjoyed at the news
the chocolates were not poisoned after all

457.
Purse-snatcher, armed gunman, a really poor liar
we sure have some world-class slim pickings here
It's killing the flirt in me

458.
buried a tin box in the yard
kept a record of the serial numbers
your guess was right, he's in for a big surprise

459.
I dropped the whole bottle of pills
in the punch bowl
our problem, plus a few others, is solved

460.
he was short, square, and bald
sprawled out flat on his back
the whole conversation took only a few minutes

461.
I took that photo
her husband is a jerk
she needs to know

462.
The back door was unlocked
I took one look and screamed my lungs out
Nothing short of decapitation will make me forget
        that sight

463.
A man murmuring into a phone
repeating the word blackmail over and over
Why yes, indeed, you'd be surprised what I know

464.
the trained chemist nosing around
ditched the shadow and took a taxi
bagged up debris behind the gas station

465.
I've been having difficulty getting to sleep
Lately so much has defied explanation
My peace of mind has been mugged.

466.
You say my accusations mean nothing
The IRS may have other ideas
it's all in the file and I made copies

467.
I was up past midnight
cried myself to sleep
who'd have thought a caper like that would go
        so wrong?

468.
there's somebody behind the sofa
just a hunch
he's not looking for dust bunnies

469.
lying on the ground
struck by lightning or hallucinations
destructive eye contact with vengeful gods

470.
the waitress in the mink coat
that girl knows everything
there's plenty in that diary of hers

471.
I quit my job today
left my shoes on the beach
under hypnosis I swam to Brazil

472.
a short stocky fellow
driving a flashy convertible way too fast
of all the guys in this city I married him

473.
chatted all evening with me
in that eerie charming manner he has
his eyes that followed me through my dreams

474.
the night clerk at the cheap hotel
talking a blue streak
on the private telephone line

475.
my memory isn't that good
I got panicky
In other words, I lied

476.
the mermaid has arrived
she could catch pneumonia in that outfit
that's the reason for all this commotion on the beach

477.
somebody must pay
by noon today or face the consequences
it's simply how extortion works

478.
the very overripe fish in the soup
the cook an accessory after the fact
no offense but next time smell it first

479.
a fatty diet, no way
the body was in terrific shape
except for being stone-cold dead

480.
it's a cash-only deal
I make off with the cash
you are stuck with the only

481.
here's a tip
this is a more sedate crowd than you're used to
tame as a box of baby pictures

482.
it's a fireworks kind of inspiration
flashes of light up in smoke
never meant to last

483.
listening to the radio at the doctor's office
the nurse cracking jokes
For a minute I forgot why I was there

484.
some people have all the luck
one of them is me
I'm as perfect and puzzling as a person's going to get.

485.
memories from a dark blue past
stabbed me in my crazy heart
sold me out and buried me

486.
extra secrets now available
at a discounted price
each a frightful story and all true.

487.
skeleton key
you'd better change clothes
put on something more law-abiding

488.
the motorcycle
screeched down the dark street
like a cat in a tough fight

489.
I've been having trouble getting to sleep
nothing's going the way positive thinking would predict
I've got heartburn like a stream of red-hot lava

490.
you shut up you big dolt
it's nothing to do with revenge
my emotions just got the better of me

491.
the doctor's diploma is a fake
the old man claws at the merest hope
a sleazy business all around

492.
the car had to be towed
we needed more time for the glue to set
a conclusion no one anticipated

493.
He's not as honest as they come
especially breezy in the early evening
yes, I fell in love with a con man

494.
poisoned champagne to celebrate
you drink it straight from the bottle
the money will be all mine very soon

495.
he doesn't socialize much he has quite a temper
jealous unkind a fraud and illiterate
I'm not running much of a dating service, am I?

496.
the heiress is running that racket
her conscience is certainly for sale
though she'd rather not do time

497.
I prefer a more egalitarian society
I facilitate sharing among members of the population
Theft is such a harsh word for my mission in life

498.
The shirt is monogrammed
MIDDLE-AGED FOOL
the guy inside it fast asleep and still talking

499.
she told you quite a yarn
a double-cross times two
an incentive-based conversation

500.
I'm willing to make a trade
your conscience for this empty purse
forgive me but they are equally uninhabited

501.
when destiny called me
there was so much yelling and pushing
I was not sure the message was for me

502.
They fingerprinted the whole family
We like to keep up with current events
but that's really getting up in our hair, I think

503.
It pains me to hear you say that
I am the stingiest lady in the whole city
I'd like to think it's more like the whole state.

504.
the adhesive on the back of drama
glues it tight to catastrophe
you can say it's trouble in a big way

505.
a fast-moving scheme a recording of a voice
sit down here and take a look at this anonymous letter
we're just about to get that blackmail thing started

506.
the two of us getting along so well
then not so much as a postcard
so I married my boss instead

507.
I am in complete agreement with the agreement
however I must strike one clause
Count me out on the poetry reading

508.
hitchhiked all the way
until he fractured his tibia
they followed him and then they caught him

509.
the accountant was really in terrible shape
he retired due to health reasons
he opened the door marked "Private"

510.
I pulled the file from the metal cabinet.
I'll ask you again
Who says you can't do business with blackmailers?

511.
Your life skidding
train wreck to nuclear meltdown
now a staged disappearance in a very expensive coat

512.
names are not important
only the knife knows its target
it will have no memory and neither will we

513.
I thought we were friends
It was a mistaken impression
The knife in the back set me straight

514.
sitting in the middle of the bus
fidgeting
thinking about doing something reckless

515.
a chronic infection of the data stream
lie after lie coming right out of your mouth
faking amnesia won't get you out of this mess

516.
your flagrant bad behavior
plus a keen amateur photographer
you little weasel, don't you think I recognized you?

517.
The portrait is so unflattering
and yet it's a very good likeness
What an unpleasant coincidence.

518.
it's all in the notebook
the picnic is my alibi
ask the ants.

519.
the imaginary playmate
I took it to the lost and found
it can't be walking around alone like this

520.
out in the snow and wearing no gloves
I don't know who I am
forgive me

521.
not so much as a postcard
from my subconscious
I don't want to be an accessory after the fact

522.
The waiter at the café
never said a word then or now
For a change I'd like to let this one go

523.
Remember your promise
double-cross times two
Twin extortion schemes just tickle me pink.

524.
your brother-in-law is not very reasonable
I can't squeeze another penny out of him
I hope I can fix things with the right tools

525.
an anonymous tip
stay away from the neighbors
they think you are an idiot.

526.
A collapsible sense of ethics
A boomerang of bad luck
She's trouble but she's my trouble

527.
a real class act you are
pushing your way through the crowd
over your quota and grabbing for more

528.
a perfectly appropriate relationship
discussing a business matter in an office
together we will make a whole lot of tax-free money

529.
My fancy new outfit and stylish hairdo
it won't be the first time you didn't pay much attention
a bunch of limp flowers won't buy you anything

530.
the parade
became an endurance test
across four states

531.
suppose I told you
I fractured his tibia
because I was not interested in the fibula

532.
in the circumstances my conscience is for sale
for the usual professional fee
now let's take a look at that will

533.
my own observations
of course that's all I can remember
they are state of the art reality

534.
the dowdy sister and the flashy sister
lipstick and a clean set of lips
so you see my dilemma

535.
your aunt
what a liar she was
designed just for that purpose

536.
the conversation is excruciating
It's likely to get worse
not yet but soon

537.
wait for instructions or don't, I sure don't care
just find out where that lunkhead went
before he breaks someone

538.
it's all good, this spy business
if you get paid on both sides of the transaction
there is plenty of travel and a large expense account

539.
it's an emergency and things are in such a jumble
first a cardiac arrest
then my phone went dead

540.
my boss was a great big wet slime
after wheezing out especially noxious gases
a specialist had to be called in

541.
I thought my luck would hold out a little longer
things went so wrong
what an awful smell

542.
Keeping tabs on you
He's not a jealous husband
just a husband interested in blackmail

543.
Crystal ball
I'm afraid it's not good news
Hey man, look out for the bus.

544.
I met you a million years ago
back in your ambiguous past
when you had a kitchen full of empty soy sauce bottles

545.
talk about lack of imagination
the worst-kept secret in this town
and it was a complete shock to me

546.
I intend to develop a connection
between me and the black beaded evening dress
I think it could be arranged via credit card

547.
employed as a personal shopper
I de-escalate figure flaws and fashion folly
for people with a lot of ready cash

548.
fine, keep your secrets
you make your own choices
but even the chickens are suspicious

549.
Threw a surprise party
turned into a sobriety sing-a-long
Set the chairs in a circle and join in!

550.
got her bags packed and put her on the bus
gave her a new purse with money in it
now you tell me the whole plan is in tatters

551.
I've been whistling for almost an hour
out there in the weeds
and all you say is: More gratitude, less complaining

552.
a coup in progress
and all you say is:
I need to call my babysitter

553.
Hit in the head with a tree branch
I was dead until three days ago.
it's not surprising that I've lost perspective.

554.
We played music. We hoped.
I told you we'd be safe.
Two people who wanted the same thing.

555.
I like the way it looks
that signet ring on your little finger.
I hope my flattery will expedite your capitulation.

556.
Old friend blackmailing you?
It won't hurt you
now that you are divorced.

557.
What I've done
I'm ashamed of it.
Remember. I think he remembers.

558.
The stars align.
The nameless conjuror comes to town.
Let's gear up for some top-drawer mayhem.

559.
nuts bolts scrap metal
the electricity in the humid air
I sense stunning opportunities ripe for the picking.

560.
I guess I got in too deep
I don't want to spend the rest of my life in jail
I'm just a librarian with wicked research skills

561.
maybe just maybe
I'm not ready to become a demon yet
but I think my twin sister is

562.
a man carrying a bag of dirty laundry
don't worry it's not radioactive
though it's most certainly toxic

563.
I wish I could act a little more human
please accept my apologies and my saddest
        facial expression
I was just indulging in a little lawyer humor.

564.
People, I'm going to lie to you:
No one needs to know.
You can get away with just sending flowers.

565.
don't you get pushy with me now
I'm a demon's daughter
a snap of my fingers and your hair is on fire

566.
Via the efforts of a competent hit man
he took a permanent nap on the living room floor
a hundred cleanings will not save that rug

567.
I went out and had a couple of beers
I thought he had double-crossed me
He was my best friend.

568.
take a yellow pill
it's hard not to
this show must go on

569.
several years into this existence
the one I paid for in cash
I no longer have a great deal of patience

570.
a paradox: agoraphobic claustrophobe
conclusive proof
that a person can turn himself inside out and
        back again

571.
multiple layers of inattention
a cheap wristwatch gone dead
honked the horn twice no go
a nice white shirt scorched with a too-hot iron

572.
of course I'm a damn good wife
I learned how
from a TV commercial

573.
a very simple lock
a skilled typist
this is all it will take to ruin the family's reputation

574.
it was a hit and run accident
two thousand miles above the earth
one of the asteroids was not wearing its glasses

575.
he denies he belongs to the country club
he doesn't have any fingerprints to speak of
he's a cool customer all right

576.
a phony alibi
add it up
I'm the bait, am I?

577.
now you know where I stand
I'm just a heartsick housewife
my husband a malodorous slob

578.
she's a liar and she's practicing it right now
amnesia is such a handy tool
she's been rehearsing that scene for weeks

579.
that surplus electrical equipment
I did have safety concerns
but you are the one screaming

580.
heroin and bets on horseracing
It's not a healthy way to spend our spare time
let's get a bridge game going instead.

581.
the young man has been hypnotized
by that very successful woman
My wife.

582.
Oh, and I stole a little money from the bank
There's no proof plus it's so embarrassing
That's why I don't want to mention it

583.
The city limits are coming up soon
Let's scare up a little more speed out of this old beater
As long as bees have teeth we're good and gone

584.
how good is your hearing?
exactly how nosy are your neighbors?
What kind of questions are those?

585.
I had a late lunch
I had to test-fire the moon rocket
Between you and me
we'd get better results from a meat thermometer

586.
He's a real playboy albeit a tame one
the whole family was in a stew
over that little problem with the hush money

587.
soul crushers
you know who they are
you know who is behind all of this

588.
I'm 100% certain
I'm in a state of shock
I thought you'd died of old age a long time ago

589.
a black eye and a split lip
photographer or lawyer take your pick
I'm plenty embarrassed already

590.
finally, I figured it out sitting on the front porch
at two o'clock in the morning
I look great in this picture, don't I?

591.
skimpy dialogue and off-key humming
you're going to have to expect skepticism
hope that movie-goers leave their eyes and ears
        at home

592.
something between a shuffle and a click
I was so startled that I jumped back and fell
landed in the bank vault on a big pile of cash

593.
look here at this crowbar
I won it in a card game
Took it off my twin sister.☐

594.
It could be fake it could be real
I've been so confused
That's why I'm so confusing

595.
Holiday visitors
Half-familiar faces around the dinner table
Some sort of parasitic invasion all right

596.
Me: Was it some kind of blackout
Him: I'll see if I can find a light switch
Me: It wasn't that kind of blackout

597.
I have the largest collection
of boyfriend problems
on the east coast

598.
I put my trust in a fifth-rate personal shopper
now I'm dressed like an uptight soccer mom
keeping secrets

599.
is a host-parasite relationship
my preferred domestic arrangement?
I'm not saying yes and I'm not saying no

600.
I've spent years of my life trying to explain it
this souvenir of that insane night
but it made a lot of sense at the time.

601.
it was clearly a professional hit
she was all business
she indisposed her neighbor with that toxic cherry pie

602.
crime on a frozen afternoon
the empty cold future
hiding behind a gravestone

603.
I'm giving you an ultimatum
don't put that money through the shredder
or I'll push you in after it

604.
Tying me up and leaving me
with a half-rotted cantaloupe on my head
that's what I consider an affront

605.
the facts are plain
the wedding ring was too tight
and you had no intention of catching that plane

606.
I cleaned out the savings account
stopped going to therapy
bought a whole new wardrobe
I think we're square now.

607.
Holy cottage cheese salad
What a messed-up-looking pile of calories
laid out exhausted on that plate

608.
I'm so shaken
I ask myself, what did I miss?
Will I ever get back my dignity?

609.
a fine example of a parsimonious husband
on the way to the office
intoxicated with his own perfection

610.
there's an awful lot of money in that wallet
I think we can come to an arrangement
oh please don't grovel

611.
ruin
unfair advantage
heartbreak
Let me catch you up with everything that's happened.

612.
it was the most squalid kitchen you've ever seen
it had a monopoly on utter and complete noxious grime
I took a peek and wished I hadn't

613.
remind me how lucky I am
I had no idea. Wild idea.
Who gave you that idea?

614.
it's just that she's such a big liar
now it's time to set a lid on that pot
Hope she doesn't boil over

615.
remember the last time you wore this dress
I said it then I'll say it now
authentic fact — glitter looks good on you

616.
Hello my darling, my pawn
Outrageous profiteering
How much I love this business!

617.
Can I believe anything you're telling me
what if what we're doing is illegal
and did you say prawn or pawn?

618.
the nurse and her patient
a magnifying glass
and all she did was tell the truth

619.
A blood feud
it will take a little bit of time
but the chatter is you're ready to atone

620.
Now I'm not smart.
I was jitters.
Know. Him. Not.
Husband enough. Father. No.

621.
from the plane
I could see the earth way below me
gossip and public opinion meaningless and absurd

622.
you've gone to all that trouble
four hundred attempts
I have zero shame in telling you that I still don't care.

623.
can two people have identical thumbprints?
what sort of flim-flam scheme
is your mother pushing?

624.
we all walk restless and still surviving
but did you ever stop to think it's finite
flung aside with ease?

625.
how kind of you to come here and gloat
my four-star enemy
I'll eat the poisoned apple if you will

626.
you signed a confidentiality agreement
but I can just smell those secrets
Six motels and taking the bus back home?

627.
Burn chocolate
Melt noodles
Blowtorch your hair
Shut you up.

628.
a real donnybrook going on upstairs
she had no ID and couldn't remember her name
for Pete's sake it was just a baby tooth

629.
I rang the doorbell
I married the rich guy who answered
It seemed quite logical at the time

630.
that sure wasn't much of a funeral
he sure wasn't much of a friend
smug little creep

631.
Marbles for eyes
String for hair
I heard that everyone was punished.

632.
Ill-timed emotions
I provoke and I never apologize
I simply don't have the temperament for it.

633.
the professor's research is simply fabulous
wig and lipstick and I'm a different person
it's called the gray oatmeal therapy

634.
Bromance?
thanks
but no thanks and no thanks and get lost

635.
Because I am hungry,
the doctor said,
ominously omnivorously.

636.
Keep my mother away from that party
You learn how to worry
when you're the child of a parent

637.
you fell in love
you hit the ground hard
walk away you're not ready

638.
malleable questioner
incompetent jury
you tell me what the verdict is

639.
kinetic locksmith
affluent framework
yeah, it's another shakedown

640.
free fall in the sky
yank the cord with your teeth
hoping for a little slowdown

641.
caramel decision
sticky situation
all done and cleaned up

642.
you only you
very cuddly
crazier than the nuts on the tree

643.
kissing the cat
and what is her name
and what are the long-term effects?

644.
Messenger in a bee cloak
carry this appeal:
Miracle needed.

645.
a lot of positive aggression right here
I saw that brick go through the window
I'm sure that made somebody feel better

646.
Gorgeous haywire indignation
You'd better save up your energy
for a conversation with her

647.
Kickback laggard?
Nothing is sure except
death and the bagman

648.
twins of course
looped in denial
are we surrendering or surviving?

649.
a chain smoker
working off the books
a self-made shyster

650.
on stage
nervous energy in front of pink sparkly lights
glassy-eyed

651.
talk talk talk talk talk all afternoon
I am a hostage looking for escape
a squirming worm on a hook

652.
I went to that wedding
I smiled so big that it hurt
Now leave me be with my exhaustion and regret

653.
we are not living on a medieval farm
a holy hermit in a cave
just outside our front door

654.
we were so in love
it was a real head-scratcher
why did I ever want a ride on this merry-go-round?

655.
secretive yellow x-ray eyes
a ghost living out here in the suburbs
the toxin was so effective and tasted so good

656.
sweet-talked the doctor
a nose job done in innovative fashion
with a brand-new set of knives

657.
your language it's a serious health issue
gave my granny a heart attack
and me a week of bad dreams

658.
please be happy about things
give me a big big big smile
lots of self-medication going on

659.
Be three eyes
Be just that one true thing
Be luminous

660.
Paper cutter meet jackhammer
reckless and spendthrift
throws that slicing power around

661.
Go home Mister Not.
All-time prize of a boyfriend
I'm not sure if you're even alive
or just wrapped in waxed paper

662.
falling asleep on the sofa
one of the symptoms
the syndrome infecting one hundred and three persons

663.
the hawk in the mist
the air inside each raindrop
there is never perfect clarity

664.
divide and then subtract
everything comes back
but always the network has a few gaps

665.
you
with the receding chin
answer the question

666.
the interior decorator
robbed your home's personality
fenced it to a house down the block

667.
the elevator is moving too fast
upward mobility
chewed up the paycheck

668.
strangers in such odd places
we dress up for the formal dinner
microscopic robots polishing the silverware

669.
this is not a good life
trimmed too close to the edge
cut me out of the action

670.
shhh no secrets
look into my brilliant blue eyes
spill them

671.
not a surrender
because I will push back
my antipathy will pay off

672.
sure there were good reasons
well, good for me
because I'm the boss I win again

673.
You made me stomp on my own self
there will be nothing left of my head
when you're finished with it

674.
the self-made shyster who raised you
is she trustworthy or not?
I don't even know why I'm asking

675.
the knees ached in the cold
the roses died in winter
I pushed too hard.

676.
so what stopped you
just in the nick of time
was it a bear or an ogre?

677.
I am a worm who just avoided the hook
breathe in breathe out breathe in breathe out
pretend it never happened

678.
you are going to hear from my lawyer all right
you served a search warrant on me
at the church fair

679.
You are wrapped up in that whole circus
Put on your brainwave costume
Let's hear your idea

680.
I'm not a terrible liar
I was a quick study
I got good at it and fast

681.
Dangerous hasn't missed a day of work
would you like to see a menu
or let her select for you

682.
clipped my fingernails
at the dinner table
oh yeah I did do that

683.
it's a wolfman's baby tooth
beautiful
in a small desiccated way

684.
relentless credit cards
struggling to get out of the wallet
Can you stop your purse from exploding?

685.
I'm just curious
I ask you point-blank
Was your inheritance as small as I think?

686.
an old soul
I'm proud of my antique identity
I've never been a teenager out late on a school night

687.
I've never been squeamish
It's just that I hate fondue
the smell is nothing short of putrid

688.
the bad apples
from the organic horror storybook
pile on some drama

689.
you wrote that book
insane disordered prose that made my skin crawl
erased every wrinkle on my body

690.
kind woman
she is the real guacamole
dished out in a Tupperware bowl

691.
I paid up to the end of the year
you cannot deny me
my turn to speak to the oracle

692.
when you leave well-enough alone
the fading truth
cannot extinguish the denial

693.
magnetic and no friction
strong alkaline taste
everything a good lemon cake ought to be

694.
connect the dots
it sure would speed things up
if you'd just go ahead and blame me

695.
sure let's tell a few jokes the boss said
as much as you don't want to hear them
Let's get familiar with exploitation

696.
here it is, a decision to make
you have everything but a sink full of soapsuds
and you want that too?

697.
you haven't been poisoned yet have you?
I do see nine obituaries waiting for ten
if my crystal ball is correct.

698.
let's say I hate mean and stupid
let's say I hate small-minded
I maybe sometimes have a problem telling the truth
This is not one of those times.

699.
my daughter
I have no influence on her
it's the one thing that eludes me

700.
my anti-fatigue strategies:
unstoppable house-cleaning
never answering the phone

701.
pile on some respect and camaraderie
it's always worth a try I guess
in any office environment

702.
are you ready to forgive yourself
accept things as they are
steer yourself back home?

703.
oh tarnation look what has happened
so sorry you're in the mess you're in
but when it's too late well it's too late

704.
ease out into the traffic
streets washed by the blue moonlight
it's late it's maybe too late

705.
sure, all dancers are agile
but
I'm a human being not a lizard

706.
a creative person
doesn't reject those purple thoughts
sews them into a slinky evening dress instead

707.
who is this creature
who is so rude
who took me on the most exciting motorcycle ride ever

708.
I've been partying for days
you don't have to yell
I hear you fine

709.
all I know is never become a spider
unless a mincing hurried shuffle
comes naturally to you

710.
I've received some technical questions about the
        eyeliner tube
I'm sure it's a coded message
Spin it around backwards and see what it says

711.
now I'm powerless to buy him off
you don't have to worry
the jalapenos will do the job just fine

712.
a few splendid things
stylish and polished
break the spell

713.
I'm repentant
I still have a human soul
running out of time just like you

714.
When everything died in the greenhouse
it was not evil spirits
it was the name-calling and the insults

715.
egalitarian foolishness in the office
what is the world coming to
when we all have cubicles of the same size?

716.
what other syllables will I speak
when the rhythms call my name
and the leaves blow in the breeze?

717.
salty language
from the kindergarten class
learning to tie their shoes

718.
portrait
of old age
leaning in a corner

719.
from the observatory
got a clear view of plastic shopping bags
floating in space

720.
in bright sunlight
sprawled in the chair
thinking scintillating thoughts

721.
You go right ahead and hope
But to make it very plain:
No chance, it will never be you

722.
tone of that day
white and colorless
self-portrait of a too-rational friend

723.
Only the moon in the sky
wondering whether to tell
in its slow second swing around the sky

724.
Not much could be said
because I was afraid
and it was still raining

725.
carrying someone's great big head under her arm
possibilities at her fingertips
so to speak

726.
go outside and listen to yourself
the best thinking about old habits
under the open sky and stars

727.
it took a glass eye and a lot of bravery
skinny legs and a pair of chartreuse pants
to ski down that great big mountain

728.
do you happen to know a good handyman
emotive and spontaneous
fully insured?

729.
we have a diva on our hands
bathrobe and plaid pajamas
custom-tailored and covered in sequins

730.
the hostile employed
a whole lot of smiling going on
a whole lot of resume-shopping going on

731.
items on a menu featuring nothing special
a garish ill-fitting twosome
they've been married thirty-two years

732.
perfect timing if you want a slice of pie
only two are left
green and black

733.
A big bowl of good hot extra-spicy chili
I'm telling you to forget your diverticulitis
the psychological benefits outrun the jalapenos

734.
you call yourself a man in a mask
I would suggest you try some different approaches
the style lacking verve, in my opinion

735.
two rivals
in tears
sporting identical poodle-cut hair-dos

736.
irresistible and special, very modern
it's almost slinky
good PR is going to come out of it

737.
your overactive eyes
pure sparkle in the last three minutes
since you got a look at that big old diamond ring

738.
a veteran of starstruck
we all dream so big
it's clearly the yellow pills

739.
penalty assessed
a creative metaphor
for being made dead

740.
I told you all my darkest secrets
thought I know there is no place on earth
I can leave my guilty conscience

741.
that little troll
beyond any kind of fashion help
but what a stage presence he has

742.
nightmares and terrifying visions
hazards of such nuance
yet they have no truth to bite you with

743.
the stars in perfect balance
moving fast and covering the sky
make no mistakes

744.
too green too naïve
needed at least two extra pairs of eyes
to see what was in front of her

745.
many many icy steps
sliding fierce
brought you here

746.
loop and one more loop
make adjustments for the wind
a broken thumb spinning clockwise

747.
Let your mistakes inspire fearlessness
After that spectacular display onstage
you've got nothing left to lose

748.
recovering from pneumonia
her health an alloy of unstable elements
head lying on a pillow that's patented and
            machine washable
she's got great color and gusto

749.
articulate and you make a good appearance in photos
so you smile and pump your fist
a little bit of arm-waving and poof! you're the mayor.

750.
stay loyal to that brand of eczema cream
come on, put your heart into it
it only works if it gets clear and consistent goals and
affirmations

751.
let's go get some of these gator lips
turn up the static electricity between our ears
take off for the big city
start a brand-new life

752.
it doesn't matter if I have a pot belly
I've got plenty of air in my lungs to breathe with
if you ever need me to, I can bust down just about
        any door.

753.
I'm zero responsible
I'm not a take-charge kind of guy
I'm the original Mr. Plaid Shirt in the Back Row

754.
the flu grabbed her and threw her in bed
the fever rose ten degrees in a flash
her lungs pressed themselves out flat
I'm not sure she'll make it to the family reunion

755.
up at 2 AM mixing up a cake
a woman of vision
you skip the kitchen haggle and family hassle

756.
can you take dictation and do shorthand
type up a revelation from an anonymous source
annotate an overheard conversation?
You're hired.

757.
simple posies
the people sitting in this audience?
I think not

758.
cactus needle regrets
just grow and grow
sharper

759.
the comet asserted itself
against middle-class morality
in the middle of the night

760.
We're not a very nice family
we've gotten a taste for remote snooping
enjoying a bit of blackmail

761.
I have a purchase order here
for a peaceful hour
in a quiet place no angry no sad

762.
The plans are in my head
I hate waiting in line
how can anything possibly go awry?

763.
Stop lecturing me, he's just a guy
average perception average indifference
I worshipped him and then I didn't.

764.
not so fast sister
said the egghead in the plaid jacket
Let me handle the acetylene torch.

765.
I'm not one of them love losers
full of toxic personality traits
I'm guilty of plenty but not that.

766.
I've told you and told you
helix has nothing to do with circle or triangle
epoxy isn't going to fix that.

767.
that's a nice spin on that story
it has so many interesting characters
it's still not going to keep you out of jail

768.
such blunt words
our family reunion fell apart after about an hour
let's discuss how this is all your fault

769.
Now he's tried to steal the halo
Lucky it was stuck on with glue
This nonsense has to stop.

770.
did you come to help me I think not
you inside informant AKA snitch.
Now we need to discuss a few surprises.

771.
there's been a bit of a mix-up
the story he told he's sticking to it after all
sorry in advance for the inconvenience and legal
trouble

772.
the unpleasant truth was holding
solid and immovable
like the everlasting ice in winter

773.
there is a lady standing in our back yard
she sings bass she sings in tune
a musician that's what she says she is

774.
I get the picture
nothing will stop you
short of removing your head and destroying your brain

775.
your ex-friend
her shoulder parts
wrapped up in a serape

776.
a failed adjective
a soul banished
black pen strokes across the page

777.
your eyes are up
your eyebrows even upper
you know all of this
but you don't know all of that

778.
Yes, that house has always been too too tidy
it was just easier
to get used to the smell of ultra-bleach

779.
look at all this junk food
where did it come from
if you want a long life and pleasant retirement, confess

780.
no it's you who doesn't understand
I don't need any friends
never nudge me and think I don't notice it

781.
I'll step away and take a deep breath
I'll find another town another street another house
And don't say the word "zombie" to me ever again

782.
you and your elf genes
living under a rock like you do
of course no one would mistake you for a zombie.

783.
you lout you need to know the truth
you're more of a loser than you think you are
you're a splinter in my finger

784.
Let's lurch
patch up the gut
slow and metallic
Carbon daisy cure

785.
The map is clear
we will bypass utter chaos
on the way to the bedlam

786.
that's a real poser of a question
I never saw that one coming
I felt guilty lying to her but I did it anyway

787.
I just got so exhausted trying to make new friends
top-notch medical care
revived me

788.
a miracle in peril
Smile and make it pretty, they said,
we admire your optimism.

789.
I've never been in a coma before
nightmares and PTSD
yes.

790.
Guess what we're getting married
empty-headed as he is
radioactive as I am

791.
How long have we been married
what is taking so long
for that divorce to come through?

792.
opportunity never came to my door much less knocked
I pulled strings and they broke
I'm beginning to understand everyone dislikes me here

793.
yes, boss, I hear you
no one is plotting against you
you just need a good long rest

794.
onions die every day
ambushed in this demented world
by conscience-free herbivores

795.
the dark behind the door
the shards of glass
I do nothing but remember

796.
your selfishness is the thing I like most about you
there's a whole lot of fake people running around
you're 100% genuine unadulterated jerk

797.
I overheard your conversation with that little bird
I promised not to blackmail anyone else
I just can't resist it this one more time.

798.
What a great set of teeth you have
some clammy mushroom-white others pale gray-green
I'd say they are unique and different.

799.
the car is waiting and the man is impatient
you learned how to say good-bye in French
did you think it would hurt less?

800.
Retirement
it is a genuine terror-producing set of circumstances
I can't seem to get out of its way

801.
in due time you will learn the answer
I do feel I can share this bit of info:
not good enough just not good enough

802.
if I need money I just steal it
it's a number jumble a digit rumble
dollars looking for a ride out of town

803.
the emotional static
wiped my memory clean
I wonder if can I afford to stop running now?

804.
Normally I work alone
My alter ego spoke to me
Partner, you are safe here with me

805.
burned the lasagna on the bottom
pulled the fire alarm
there will be a big bill for damages
none of this is my fault.

806.
that anonymous tip sent me off-direction
I fell into a great big basket of hidden agenda
clacking tongues and snarled up subject lines

807.
I know you're in there you little termite
good-natured and hard-working
But I'm the one paying the mortgage.

808.
I was trying to say thank you
a broken arm was the result
do the math bottom line I'm worse off

809.
noxious fumes
the bouncer's new perfume
broke up the bar fight

810.
I never knew it would come to this you liar
I know you're an imposter
I think I like you better than the real one

811.
the downtown business district
just a pile of gray dust
what's wrong is that none of us can remember
        it anymore

812.
you've got to play along
five four three one oops forgot two
sorry but your number was two

813.
there's been all kinds of trouble in that laboratory
we traced it back now we need to
cross-baste the wires and minimize the fry-back

814.
in the shower I had a new idea
let's go down to the bus station and make a day of it
a wide range of personality traits will be on view

815.
not that it's any business of mine but
the frozen ten percent I understand
it's the stuff you left in the closet that bothers me

816.
I didn't sleep one minute last night
after that bust-up in the library yesterday
prodigious pressure group, those librarians

817.
wrap a tutu around that poodle
expect him to plié
how can anything possibly go awry?

818.
my heart
heavier than Italy
the agonizing pain
I'm madly in love with you

819.
we've got to get back on the road soon
we've lost the car deep in the mall parking lot
who says we'll ever be able to leave

820.
no long life and pleasant retirement for you
acid public opinion
corroded your stomach and your reputation

821.
standing in the hallway
I see you have a lot of space in this apartment
I'm wondering if there is a room here for me?

822.
a partnership in a consulting firm
you are the one best suited to the job
it will give your talent for meddling a focus

823.
the bank robbers torched the getaway car
it will be convalescent for a long time
if it ever recovers

824.
time to do some serious groveling
put the flowers in a vase
it's all about survival

825.
we need an inside informant AKA snitch
an unrelenting appetite for gossip
the essential skill

826.
look at all that junk food
go on over there and say hello
hurry up I think it's leaving

827.
why are you crying
it won't remove the curse
The black fog has already begun to spread

828.
my boss apologized to me
it is scaring me and it is dangerous
I just know he's got some new scheme up his sleeve

829.
this guy just saved your life
I think it's for the last time
I'm through sticking my neck out for you he said

830.
Please don't say the word "zombie"
it's an inside joke in this neighborhood
you don't ever want to find out the punch line

831.
I know first aid
I can use epoxy to fix it
I'll be double quick about it and it won't hurt at all

832.
somebody has to take the blame
let's discuss how this is all your fault
but first, did anyone call the fire department?

833.
stop pestering the man
he's strictly small-time
by the way what's he saying anyway?

834.
the house was always too tidy
it was just easier that way
I want to say I'm sorry

835.
I'll solve your little problem
I believe we could find those memories
adjust their design and composition

836.
I was unhappy and not myself
the doctors at that hospital were nice
I don't ever want to walk through that door again

837.
I learned it was all a big mistake
I was not a quick study
Boy, you sure fooled me.

838.
I'm living a life full of trouble
relieve the pressure
please come home and help me

839.
I'm a hypocrite that's what you are thinking
I'm simply telling you people are so afraid of the truth
it's more healing to leave a false impression

840.
release a rush of words
thick black pen strokes across the page
a fresh start and one good choice after another

841.
your memory
can it be pried open
redemption is not too big a word to say

842.
days weeks months
the master plan advances
one pot of boiling water at a time

843.
I have what I need, I can't pretend I don't
things change
when the calendar flips fifteen years' worth of pages

844.
I know it was only a dream
nothing but a pyramid scheme
and of course I have no medical training.

845.
the complaints started five stories up
the noise was ear-splitting
everyone wants some kind of reparations

846.
I've moved on to a new theory
align with the purple or the orange
you're not a traitor if you're nice to the right people

847.
what are you doing up so late
why are you snooping around the basement
why are you carrying around that shovel
Well, while you're here I wish you'd do the laundry

848.
I had to be extra quiet and wait
see if maybe the hive scared them off
and if not, you very bad people, I will show you
ambush.

849.
is there no light no water
in this blighted wasteland
is there nowhere to plant sunflowers?

850.
this rock
too small for the both of us
it has no greener pastures

851.
no socks no shoes no painted fingernails
yeah all of us were in on that caper
the only problem was all that snow

852.
it's the only acting job we could get
we would gladly imagine another future
a life free of incontinence commercials

853.
I had a turquoise headache
a stranger gave me a ride to the hospital
thorough city streets dense with purple buildings

854.
those people with whom you arrived
one of you will betray the others
the rest of you will be eaten at night
by that thing waiting outside in the snow.

855.
I admired your optimism logic and clear-thinking
I paid you for having a tough mind
We have never been friends and we never will be.

856.
I knew she would believe
Chances are her faith is misplaced
I think Cupid set your sister up.

857.
my alter ego spoke to me that night:
where will you ever wear this dress
why did you even try on the pink shoes?

858.
proud and regenerative
we stretch the fibers and comb them out
at the finish we sing a duet

859.
I just want to be myself
ordinary demeanor bland opinions
running naked across a basketball court

860.
yes you do owe us a lot of money
five hundred grand and that's just saying hello
this is why we have a jim-dandy tracking system

861.
is this how you make new friends
run into people with a shopping cart
get sued?

862.
Your bad luck's going to last and last
All right I'll make it simple
Indefinitely, that's how long

863.
is there anything
that will make you open your eyes
stun you with its sparkle?

864.
sure the whole world loved me
considered myself special
former employee now

865.
the investigation did not implicate any family members
we required something more personal and
          occasion-specific
accidents happen all the time

866.
plaid bathrobe and tousled hair
a danger in the kitchen
never mind I'll take care of the incinerated oatmeal

867.
steady yourself
the photographs have done a lot of damage
well, everything falls apart eventually

868.
the plates in the cabinets rattled
Together again just like old times
they've come back home

869.
a powerful loud noise she is
people listen to her
my mother the emperor

870.
I'm not a doctor of course
the funny thing is I know all the answers
Best guess is that repairs will be time-consuming

871.
memory loss is illegal in this state
second-guessing ill-luck is forbidden
naiveté will put you in jail

872.
come with me and find out why
the guy in the picture that nobody remembers
a person of interest now that it is too late

873.
speculation says to me
That flawed sense of fashion
it's going to be money in the bank

874.
the payroll is in the vault
a windfall of cash
citizens of our frayed society rise up
grab this unique opportunity

875.
I'll make myself useful I don't hold grudges
Go ahead believe it
I'm loving seeing you being played

876.
I think I'm just getting started
In bed and in a happy deep slumber
lots of good dreams to choose from

877.
ochre wind glows
risk green wavers in acid yellow sky
silver stars shatter indigo clouds

878.
my name was not important
my number was nineteen
not at first but later

879.
we are no more friends
than we are jars of peanut butter
there is zilch zero not a hint of a chance of a sandwich

880.
push the button
pay out that rope
you've got no idea why you just did this do you

881.
pushed him out of the airplane
dropped him on his head
Boy did that change his mind

882.
the floor waxer
took the scenic route
traveled the linoleum between pale blue walls

883.
You paid to send me on a string of wild
        inner-space trips
yell if you need me you said so I said
things are spooky charming and expensive but I'm fine
        so far

884.
our business relationship
your artistic freedom
maybe some other time

885.
just between us
you may want to reconsider
because what if mind control is real?

886.
what if face-saving isn't possible
what if there is a jinx on the whole operation
what if it's a classic fork strike-back?

887.
I guess I'm running late again
One last emergency
I promise

888.
I am one of those bad people
doing things she should be sorry about
but is not

889.
listen to yourself hard-headed like concrete
you say you've been here before
doing the same stupid thing

890.
the old memory
that's the key for this lock
now stand clear as I open the door

891.
a thousand little guys pushing too hard
weighing their costs
coming off second best

892.
The Atypical Meatloaf
there is always a chemical taste
it's nothing to worry about

893.
You give up that morsel of radioactive energy
every day will start to look alike
your party clothes will no longer fit
any hospital in town will tell you the same thing

894.
a red firecracker
a cloud of smoke
a perfect gentleman
another wonderful evening

895.
a traitor and
none of his actions were for your benefit
yet you fell in love with him

896.
the active OK
I say it straight-line
no façade just simple yes

897.
a red herring:
the pretty little seaside cottage
standing in sparkly warm raindrops

898.
shook loose
the sugar obsession
because the time came to say goodbye

899.
can't type can only dictate memos
doesn't like anything but red meat
a classic dinosaur

900.
hurt feelings and honesty
made me want to tell
every secret I ever knew

901.
I took you to the airport
the sheriff met the eastbound bus
you owe me one.

902.
a shot of those purple antibiotics
will fix the thermostat in your liver
and get rid of your sick headache

903.
the sedative I gave you
in a cinnamon-flavored snowball
Now you will want to cooperate.

904.
close out the old accounts
wake up generous
start hoping all over again

905.
a thoroughly inferior society
I begin to doubt
any change of heart will help

906.
when will someone
take charge of that situation in the apiary
and stop calling me honey

907.
your net poised to catch him
you want him to come home
he does not want to come home

908.
the bus passengers
preparing to flee in the play's final scene
selfish of me I pushed to the front
though I knew it was only a play

909.
hey I did you a favor
I buried the bad luck in the back yard
behind the rosebushes

910.
no change of heart
a list of three names
let's finish this longstanding business

911.
my gossipy old grandma
short-sighted and avaricious
wily as a fox

912.
our selves as we used to be
don't apologize
let's just try to live a little more heart-shaped from
        now on

913.
If no one objects
I'll retreat to the laundry room
for some therapeutic irony
I mean ironing

914.
on the blind curve
you missed the gateway to sanity
opened up wide like a great big mouth

915.
announce the message
flee the drama
live in peace
dream on

916.
you need help in a hurry
call up the delivery service
ask for some ice-cold masking tape

917.
don't yank at his arm like that
just sit tight and let the dentist work
you're on his turf today

918.
a big bandage on her forehead
she's very taken with the idea of camouflage
suit yourself, I said, but we're at a swimming pool

919.
someone really is following us
just give him your return address
save him a lot of trouble

920.
who could blame you
when you ran off all the way to India
Pudgy hands and all

921.
are you seriously suggesting
my nutty family
is just about to come up with a workable scheme?

922.
the guy with the glasses
must have dozed off
it's a shame he's missing his own party

923.
the red jello came out of nowhere
clean shirt
I need it and I need it now

924.
nice job and a generous bonus
apply them to your sunburned skin
as you vacation in Fiji

925.
selfish of me it felt wrong
my conscience is bothering me
really, it was just such a little bit of ice cream

926.
I got hit on the head with a bowling trophy
in a movie theater?
is that why you brought me to the hospital?

927.
I'm a little dizzy
I think the neurotoxin has brought back my memories
and my snoring

928.
an icon
a million photos of me
But I'm a schoolteacher now.

929.
fourteen ballerinas on stage
signaled for a left turn
went wide

930.
in an awkward position
screaming
But I'm sure I'm not a ghost yet.

931.
how's the fishing here
not too good I guess
I see the barrel is empty

932.
wait just a minute, chirpy
you little paper-chewer
I don't take orders from you

933.
our getaway was so successful
people are still talking about it
so where did they find you
you old tub

934.
follow the red herring
helpless and wriggling
It might just pull this one off

935.
I'm jumpy
just like old times
my thoughts thudding around my brain's perimeter

936.
I should say not
my patience is pushed to the limit
you know how much trouble a soufflé can be

937.
you jostle up some knowledge
the whole business deal
you'll throw it right out the window

938.
now it's getting kind of breezy out there
the desiccated nostalgia
fluttering under the lights

939.
If I'm not back in two hours
you'll know I set you up as bait.
I am not honest. I never was.

940.
a mental link
with the poisonous ant
ouch it could kill me

941.
you know where but not why things went dark
you made amends
it was not enough

942.
idol status
cyanide
mixed with snide

943.
traffic jam
car marmalade
let's avoid pedestrian jelly

944.
mix concrete at faster and faster speeds
your goal
a sonic boom inside a sidewalk

945.
I sang on stage
made your ears hurt
you were real nice about it

946.
I offered forgiveness so many times
Just another way out
that's what it means to you

947.
your mind sparkles
like that jar of red jelly
but something is wrong with the flow valve

948.
escaped
or liberated
yes I am divorced

949.
I've known your secret for so long
we were friends in a previous life that's how
I didn't tell then and I won't tell now

950.
the swarm of heavily-armed yellow jackets
I knew I couldn't take one more minute in the garden
you can see it's gotten kind of complicated

951.
an electric toothbrush
knocked out your teeth?
No, it was the navy beans.

952.
the truck swerved
lots and lots of cash fell out
we're looking at a very lucrative future

953.
my guardian angel said
I don't feel helpful too often
kept an eye on the clock

954.
suspicious
tenacious
a swarm of yellow jackets on maneuvers

955.
I was just too scared
It hardly felt real
I tried it again

956.
you were too crazy
strung kind of loose
you were headed for the only exit still open
you scared me

957.
a pale shimmer in the back of my brain
like stylish champagne
another premonition

958.
driving lessons aren't cheap
french fries win no arguments
the bees sting you on your face
and for ten cents I'd eat the soap myself

959.
don't you think a tearful headache
deserves pajamas and slippers
a bowl of that fast-acting vanilla ice cream?

960.
the ball point pen
sputtered along the page
a former colleague who used to have a lot of style

961.
get some driving lessons
you almost stopped my heart
it's debatable if I'll recover from your highway
        merge technique

962.
no soap old geezer the lip man said
nobody cares about the negatives these days
when we've got the internet

963.
now where is my super-light
subtle and unstable
conscience?

964.
now seal the envelope
photos of that night
that night of dreams

965.
the old technology
never worried just believed
a long list of mystery ingredients made it work.

966.
extraordinary red color
those waterfalls
were you there on business?

967.
Remove the sticky hairspray?
I can try though maybe it's been on too long
Wave my hands poof! a puff of smoke and lady it's
    all gone

968.
we are best friends and we don't know why
the professor and I
we've checked and rechecked our calculations
we are still best friends and we still don't know why

969.
lost class notes missed exams
going through all those old papers
please! break me out of study hall

970.
so loud and you need sunglasses
there's no air like this city air
I love everything about this burg.

971.
oh no it's an emergency
multiple calls from neighbors
resident spotted wearing non-conforming sneakers

972.
green smoke in the elevator
no wife and no bridesmaids either
Leave now we can't wait until it starts to make sense

973.
point of impact my heart
you fried my electrical system with one look
I love everything about you

974.
finish the song
or skip town
just please make it stop

975.
I doubt everyone even when they swear it's the truth
It stretches my every nerve and snaps them back
          upside down
Why I became a therapist I'll never understand

976.
he was so peevish
the doctor removed his gallbladder
now he frolics like a kitten

977.
Loud blubbering and snot on your face
your dilemma I can solve
here is a small box of tissues

978.
feeling the shamefulness
a side effect
of doing something shameful

979.
classic revenge story savage and snarly
the drain in the bathtub
the innocent washcloth
the jealous rubber duck

980.
three deaths in three weeks
our family our conflicts
we solve them together

981.
stop and get a bottle of champagne
my destiny is greater than I ever dreamed
I just need a little more time to perfect my bigger ego

982.
You and your dull dry dusty intellect compiling data
you're not my cup of tea
though I like your body piercings and tattoos a lot

983.
of course I know they were valuable chickens
but salt shaker in hand it was time for dinner
leave now or join your ancestors I told them

984.
Sure I'll help you swap out your friends
I've got an elixir that will do it in a jiffy
Bon voyage to these losers.

985.
The antithesis of vulnerable
I was standing on the roof and hit by lightning
I felt just a little shiver nothing more

986.
like an unstable soufflé
wrapped up in chains
he is henpecked and loving it

987.
your life is unraveling
in that reckless I don't care kind of way
I'm giving you a ride home right now

988.
oh heck
I tuned into that basic magnetism
I'm sold

989.
what if you're not a good person
not a single flicker of good in you
but is there not a heart in each one of us?

990.
you slacker
bring it out of the shadows
start making your bed every single morning

991.
throw the dice
so that it all seems random
so that no one notices the pattern

992.
In the next cubicle
body chemistry
too powerful for ordinary soap

993.
I'm truly happy for me
I'm a social climber
experiencing a spectacular power surge

994.
I'm sick of you thinking you're smarter than anyone else
Well, you're not smarter than that chicken over there
That chicken over there is a college professor.

995.
Who said anything about
crazy goings-on at the science building
What they are doing with those vegetable peelers
        is a secret

996.
Satellite dish beams in alien signals
full of x-ray spaghetti loops
and smashed flat pronouns

997.
Take me at my word
I hope you'll understand
Try it again and you'll be table scraps

998.
while we're being honest
a mechanic and a doctor
neither one is going to cheer you up

999.
the answer to that question is always
sayonara I'm going home the long way
because there are a lot of stars in the sky

1000.
bad people doing bad things
so it was selfish and so it was easier
and so it just got to be good honest fun

1001.
that wheezing little dog
a terminally-ill refrigerator
neither of them going to last much longer

1002.
Your kitchen
a mold-growing paradise
a camping trip for easily-goaded health hazards

1003.
get the tuning fork
a disrupted nervous system
needs a little pushback now and then

1004.
let's get cracking on that dating service
I need someone to come home to
I want Valentines addressed to me

Little Vines by Date

Date	Number
4/28/17	1-13
5/5/17	14-18
5/11/17	19-34
5/17/17	35-39
5/25/17	40-50
6/1/17	51-57
6/7/17	58-71
6/22/17	72-85
6/29/17	86-96
7/5/17	97-105
7/14/17	106-117
7/20/17	118-126
7/27/17	127-144
8/3/17	145-155
8/10/17	156-169
8/17/17	170-180
8/23/17	181-194
8/31/17	195-215
9/7/17	216-232
9/13/17	233-249
9/21/17	250-265
9/28/17	266-278
10/5/17	279-292
10/12/17	293-307
10/20/17	308-328
10/27/17	329-354
11/2/17	355-377
11/9/17	378-393

11/16/17	394-412
11/22/17	413-429
11/30/17	430-447
12/7/17	448-465
12/14/17	466-489
12/21/17	490-507
12/28/17	508-530
1/3/18	531-548
1/11/18	549-565
1/18/18	566-593
1/25/18	594-608
2/1/18	609-634
2/9/18	635-662
2/15/18	663-691
2/22/18	692-717
3/1/18	718-755
3/8/18	756-783
3/15/18	784-816
3/23/18	817-848
3/30/18	849-877
4/5/18	878-908
4/12/18	909-938
4/19/18	939-975
4/26/18	976-1004